The World of Plants

How Plants Grow

Carrie Branigan
and Richard Dunne

W
FRANKLIN WATTS

First published in 2005 by Franklin Watts
96 Leonard Street, London EC2A 4XD

Franklin Watts Australia
45-51 Huntley Street, Alexandria, NSW 2015

© Franklin Watts 2005

Editor: Rachel Cooke
Art director: Jonathan Hair
Designer: Michael Leaman Design Partnership
Line illustrations by Jeremy Leaman
Consultant: Gill Matthews

A CIP catalogue record for this book
is available from the British Library

ISBN 0 7496 5580 1

Printed in Malaysia

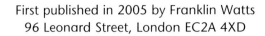

Contents

Plants All Around

Look around you when you go for a walk. It won't be long before you spot a plant.

You see plants in gardens and parks.

▲ Many plants have brightly coloured **flowers**.

You see plants along streets and roads.

▶ Plants grow along the sides of this motorway.

You even see plants growing through cracks in the pavement.

◀ Weeds are plants that grow where they are not wanted.

With an adult, take a 10-minute walk from your home or school. Count how many plants you see.

Parts of a Plant

There are many different types of plant. Most of them grow **flowers**.

Flowering plants come in all shapes and sizes. They have the same parts.

▲ You can see this plant's flower, **leaves**, **stem** and **roots**. Normally, its roots are hidden in the soil.

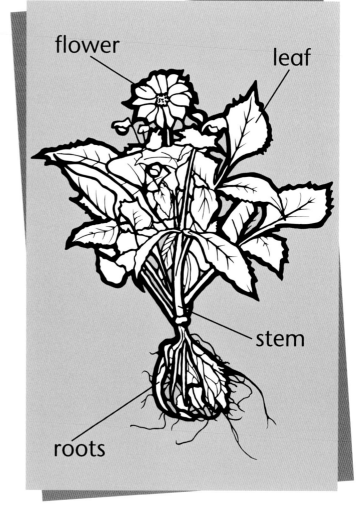

flower

leaf

stem

roots

We call the stem of a tree its trunk. Its branches are side stems.

leaves

branch

▶ The roots reach out underground from the bottom of the tree trunk.

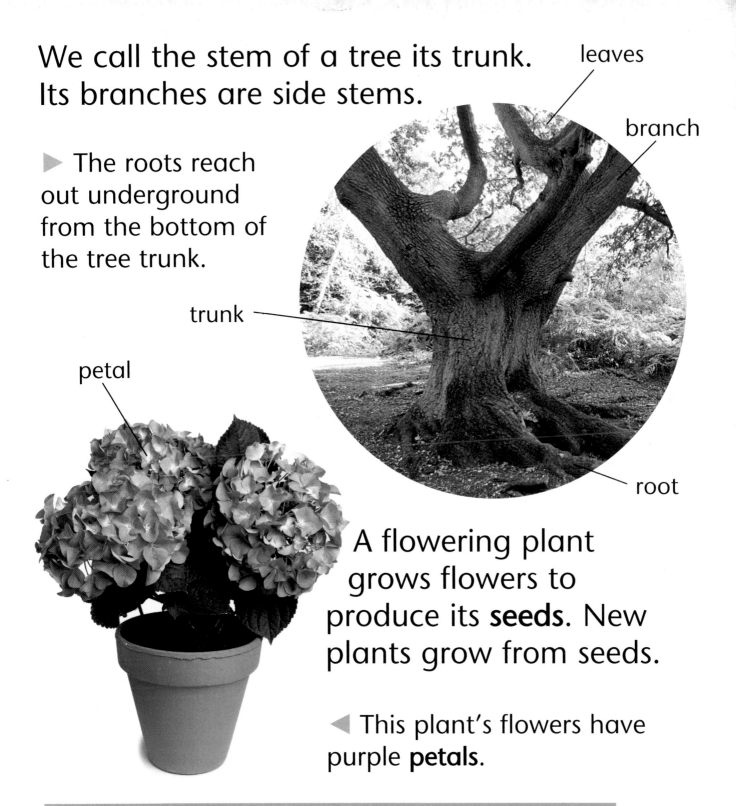

trunk

petal

root

A flowering plant grows flowers to produce its **seeds**. New plants grow from seeds.

◀ This plant's flowers have purple **petals**.

Look at a tree, a pot plant and a weed. Look out for their stems and leaves. Why is it hard to see their roots? Do they have flowers?

9

Growing and Changing

Just like animals, plants grow and change as they get older.

A new flowering plant starts life as a **seed**. First it grows a **root** and then a **shoot**.

leaves

shoot

stem

seed (bean)

root

▲ This is a young bean plant. Bean plants grow from seeds called beans. You can still see the bean the plant grew from.

Then the plant grows taller with more **leaves**. Later it grows **flowers** and then produces seeds.

flower

pod

▲ These bean plants are fully grown. Some of the flowers have produced seeds. The seeds are held inside **pods**.

Look at the pictures on the outside of some seed packets. Then look at the seeds inside. These seeds will grow into the plants shown on the packet!

Life Times

Flowering plants have different lengths of life time. This is the time they take to grow, make their seeds and die.

Some plants grow, produce their **seeds** and die in a year. We call these plants **annuals**.

▶ A marigold is an annual, so is a bean plant (see page 10).

Some plants live for two years. They are called **biennials**.

◀ A foxglove is a biennial. It grows **leaves** and stores food in its first year. In the second year, it **flowers** and produces its seeds.

Some plants live for many years.
These plants are called **perennials**.

Some perennials have **bulbs**. Bulbs are underground food stores made of a swollen **stem** and leaves.

flower

leaves

bulb

root

▲ Crocuses have bulbs. They grow new flowers and leaves each year. These die but more grow again from the bulb the next year.

As soon as they are large enough, most perennials produce seeds every year.

Do you think trees are perennials?

How Roots Work

A plant's **roots** hold it in the ground.
The roots also take in water.
The plant needs water to grow.

As a plant grows bigger, so do its roots They grow because they have to take in more water and help the plant to stand up.

◀ The roots of this tree stretch out under the ground as widely as its branches do above.

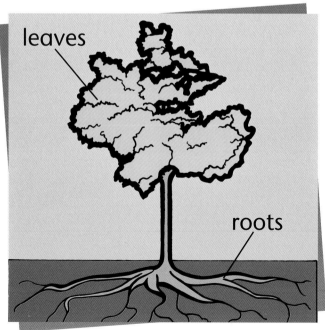

leaves

roots

What do you think would happen to a tall plant on a windy day if it didn't have strong roots?

Plants grow better if their roots have enough room to grow.

▲ This pot plant's roots are tangled and squashed. It needs to be put in a bigger pot.

◄ A gardener has planted these carrots so their roots have plenty of space. The plants are growing well.

Plants and Water

Water from the **roots** passes up the **stem** to the **leaves** and **flowers** of the plant.

Plants that don't get enough water begin to **wilt**. Without water they will die.

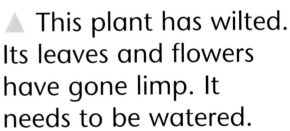

▲ This plant has wilted. Its leaves and flowers have gone limp. It needs to be watered.

◀ The plant has now been watered. It is growing well again.

veins

flower

leaf

Water moves through plants in a network of tubes called **veins**.

◄ There are veins in the stem, leaves and flowers. The thickest veins are in the stem.

Use some food dye to colour a glass of water. Put a celery stick in the water and let it stand for a few hours. Cut through the celery. Can you see the coloured water in the celery's veins?

Leaves Make Food

Leaves do an important job for the plant. They make its food. Food gives plants energy to grow.

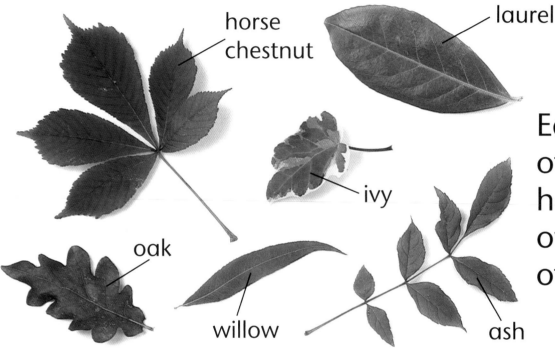

horse chestnut

laurel

ivy

oak

willow

ash

Each type of plant has its own type of leaf.

oak leaf

◀ Some leaves have only one part to them.

▶ Other leaves have several smaller parts called leaflets.

ash leaf

a leaflet

The water in leaves mixes with a gas from the air. The plants use sunlight to change this mixture into food.

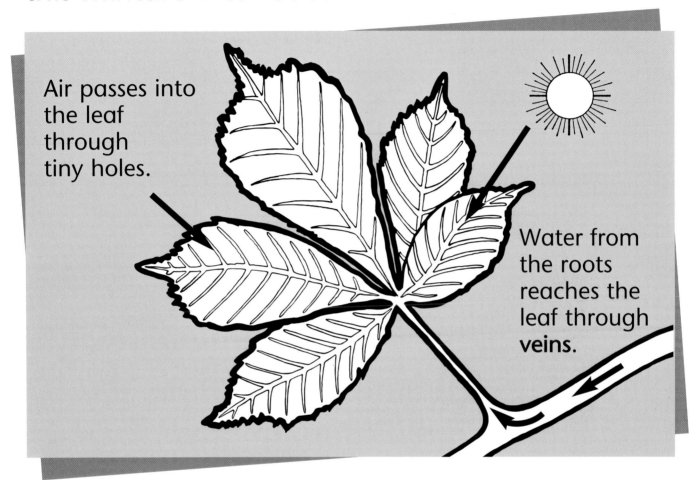

Air passes into the leaf through tiny holes.

Water from the roots reaches the leaf through **veins**.

▲ The way plants make their food is called **photosynthesis**.

We can't make food for ourselves in the same way as plants. What do we do to get our food?

Plants grow using the food they make. Some plants store food to use later.

Plants and Light

All plants need light to grow.
Without light they can't make their food.

A plant starts to grow in the dark soil using a store of food in its **seed**.

Its first **leaves** push up to the light. Now the plant can make food to grow bigger.

Plants' leaves grow so each leaf gets as much light as possible.

▶ Each leaf on this plant catches some light.

Plants grow towards the light. Some even turn on their **stem** to follow the Sun.

▲ Sunflowers turn to follow the Sun across the sky.

Plants kept in the dark lose their green colour. They grow thin and spindly.

◀ This seedling has been kept in the dark for a few days.

Put a tray on a piece of lawn and leave it for a few days. Take the tray off and see what has happened to the grass beneath it.

Flowers and Seeds

Plants grow **flowers** so that new plants can grow. The flowers produce the plants' **fruits** and **seeds**.

flower bud

pollen

flower

petal

First **buds** grow. Then the buds open and the **petals** open out.

Inside flowers is a powder called **pollen**.

Pollen has to move from one flower to another for the seeds to form.

▲ Some plants' pollen is moved by the wind.

▲ Other plants' pollen is moved by animals, usually insects.

After **pollination**, the flowers produce fruits. Inside the fruits are the seeds.

▶ Courgettes are fruits. Inside them are seeds.

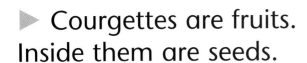

Cut open some fruit you eat. Can you find the seeds?

Through the Seasons

In the parts of the world where there are cold winters, plants grow and change with the seasons.

◀ During the winter, **seeds** and **bulbs** stay safe under the ground. Only a few plants keep their **leaves** all year round. They are called evergreens.

◀ Plants start to grow in spring when the weather gets warmer. New **shoots** appear and new leaves open out.

During the hot summer, many **flowers** open. The **pollen** in the flowers is moved to other flowers by insects.

In the autumn, most trees lose their leaves. Seeds are scattered by the wind and by animals eating **fruit**.

Draw pictures of a park or garden in each of the four seasons. Think of how all the different plants will look.

Helping Plants Grow

Gardeners and farmers do lots of things to help plants grow strong and healthy.

They make sure the plants get enough water, light and air to grow properly.

◀ Grape vines are planted on sunny hillsides. Farmers give them plenty of water.

When **roots** collect water, they also take in tiny amounts of minerals from the soil that help the plant grow.

▶ Gardeners add **compost** to the soil to make sure it has plenty of minerals in it.

Many plants grow better in warm places. Cold weather like frost can kill some plants.

◀ A greenhouse helps plants grow more quickly. It also protects plants from cold weather.

Keep a pot plant or grow some **seeds** inside. What do you need to do to help your plants grow? Where is a good place to put them?

Amazing Facts

Some of the largest leaves grow on the Amazonian bamboo palm from South America. The leaves can measure up to 20 metres long.

A type of bamboo found in India and Asia grows very fast. It can grow 91 cm in a day. It grows to a height of about 37 metres.

The longest roots ever measured belonged to a fig tree growing in South Africa. Its roots reached over 120 metres into the ground.

Use your book to find the answers to this Amazing Plants quiz!

- What are the different parts of a plant called?

- Why do some plants grow flowers?

- How do a plant's roots help it to grow?

- Why do plants need sunlight?

- What is the stem of a tree called?

- How does a plant get minerals from the soil?

- What are bulbs?

Glossary

annual a flowering plant that grows, flowers, produces seeds in one year and then dies.

biennial a flowering plant that takes two years to grow, flower, produce seeds and die.

bud a flower or leaf before it opens.

bulb a part of some plants, a bulb is a swollen stem surrounded by layers of leaves that stores food and grows underground.

compost rotting leaves, grass and plants used to improve the soil.

flower part of a flowering plant that makes its fruits and seeds. Flowers are often very colourful.

fruit part of a plant that grows from the flower and protects the seeds.

leaf part of a plant that is usually green. The leaf uses sunlight, air and water to make food for the plant.

minerals substances that are found naturally in the ground which plants need to grow.

perennial a flowering plant that lives for many years.

petals outer parts of a flower that are often colourful.

photosynthesis the way plants make their food in their leaves.

pod a type of fruit of some plants, such as bean plants.

pollen a fine powder made by flowers. Pollen needs to move from one flower to another for seeds to form.

pollination the movement of pollen from one flower to another.

roots part of a plant that holds the plant in the soil. The roots take up water from the soil.

seed seeds are made in the flower of a flowering plant. When seeds are planted, new plants grow from them.

shoot new growth on a plant, in particular the first stem and leaves it grows.

stem part of a plant that holds up the leaves and flowers and connects them with its roots.

veins thin tubes that carry water and food around a plant.

wilt to go limp and droopy.

Index